Greek Mythology

The Definitive Beginner's Guide to the Gods and Heroes of Ancient Greece

Graves May

Table of content

Chapter 1: Introduction to Greek Mythology..5
   - Overview of Greek mythology and its importance in ancient Greek culture 5
   - The role of myths in ancient societies and their impact on modern culture 8
   - The sources of Greek mythology and their reliability..10

Chapter 2: The Creation Myth..14
   - The creation of the universe according to Greek mythology 14
   - The roles of Chaos, Gaia, Uranus, and Cronus..16
   - The birth of the Olympian gods and goddesses 19

Chapter 3: The Olympian Gods and Goddesses...23
   - An overview of the Olympian gods and goddesses 23
   - Their roles and domains of influence 26
   - Famous myths featuring the Olympians, such as the abduction of Persephone 29

Chapter 4: Heroes and Mortals..33
   - The role of heroes and mortals in Greek mythology 33
   - Famous heroes such as Hercules, Achilles, and Theseus 36
   - The concept of the hero's journey and its significance in Greek mythology 38

Chapter 5: Monsters and Creatures 43
   - The role of monsters and creatures in Greek mythology..43
   - Famous examples such as the Minotaur, Medusa, and the Hydra 46
   - The symbolism and significance of these creatures in Greek mythology....................48

Chapter 6: The Trojan War 53
   - The story of the Trojan War and its importance in Greek mythology...........................53
   - The key players, such as Achilles, Agamemnon, and Hector.....................................55
   - The aftermath of the war and its impact on Greek mythology 59

Chapter 7: Love and Relationships 63
   - The role of love and relationships in Greek mythology 63
   - Famous examples such as the love story of Orpheus and Eurydice...........................66
   - The symbolism and significance of these stories in Greek mythology.......................68

Chapter 8: The Underworld 73
   - The Greek concept of the afterlife and the underworld 73
   - The role of Hades, Persephone, and Charon in Greek mythology 75

   - Famous myths featuring the underworld, such as the story of Orpheus and Eurydice............................78

Chapter 9: The Twelve Labors of Hercules *83*

   - The story of Hercules and his twelve labors 83

   - The symbolism and significance of these labors in Greek mythology....................................86

   - The impact of Hercules on Greek mythology and culture 90

Chapter 10: The Legacy of Greek Mythology *94*

   - The enduring legacy of Greek mythology in modern culture 94

   - The influence of Greek mythology on literature, art, and popular culture 97

   - Reflections on the importance of Greek mythology in understanding human nature........................100

Chapter 1: Introduction to Greek Mythology

- Overview of Greek mythology and its importance in ancient Greek culture

Greek mythology is a huge and intricate body of ideas and tales that were essential to ancient Greek culture and worldview. The natural world, people, and the enigmas of the cosmos were all explained by these tales. Greek mythology's tales were passed down orally through the ages and subsequently written down, where they have persisted in captivating and fascinating people for millennia.

Greek mythology's influence on ancient Greek culture and society is among its most significant characteristics. The moral lessons and cultural norms and values were reinforced through the employment of myths. For instance, it's common to read the myth of Prometheus, who stole fire from the gods and gave it to humans, as a warning against disobedience and rebellion. Similar to this, the legend of Icarus, who perished after flying too close to the sun, serves as a warning against the perils of ambition and hubris.

Ancient Greek religious customs were significantly influenced by Greek mythology. In temples and sanctuaries all around the Greek world, the gods and goddesses of Greek mythology were worshipped, and offerings and sacrifices were given to them in an effort to win their favor. Many of the tales were reenacted during religious festivals and ceremonies, and they were used to explain the procedures and practices of devotion.

Greek mythology's tales were significant for their entertainment appeal in addition to their religious and moral relevance. People of all ages and all groups delighted in the myths, which were frequently repeated in open spaces like fairs or the marketplace. The tales frequently included music and dancing, and they were rife with drama, passion, and adventure.

Greek mythology's impact on Western society and literature is another significant factor. The myths have served as inspiration for some of the greatest pieces of writing and art in human history and have been repeated and altered countless times in literature, art, and popular culture. Greek mythology's ideas and motifs are still relevant to people today, and the tales continue to inspire and fascinate people of all ages.

In summary, Greek mythology is a deep and intricate system of philosophies and narratives that was fundamental to ancient Greek culture and society. The myths, which still enthrall and inspire people today, have been utilized to impart moral lessons, explain natural occurrences, and influence religious rituals. Greek mythology continues to be a crucial component of our cultural history, whether it is being read for leisure, studied as literature, or utilized to investigate human nature.

- The role of myths in ancient societies and their impact on modern culture

Ancient societies relied heavily on myths to help them make sense of their surroundings and to explain natural events that their primitive scientific understanding was unable to explain. In addition to reinforcing social norms and beliefs, myths also acted as a means of transferring cultural traditions and values from one generation to the next.

Myths were a major component of religion in ancient Greece and were used to explain the deities' and heroes' motivations. Greek gods and heroes' legends continue to be well-known in contemporary society, inspiring works of art, literature, and even contemporary superhero tales. The stories of gods like Zeus, Apollo, and Athena have evolved into iconic and enduring emblems of strength, power, and wisdom. Greek mythology's themes and motifs are still relevant to audiences today.

In addition to providing amusement, myths were used by ancient societies to instill moral values. While cautionary tales like that of Narcissus forewarned against the pitfalls of vanity and self-absorption, stories of heroes like Hercules and Theseus were used to teach virtues like bravery, tenacity, and self-sacrifice. These teachings are still applicable today, and Greek mythological themes are continually being researched and reexamined in modern literature and popular culture. Additionally, myths have had a significant impact on modern literature and language. The archetypes and motifs of ancient mythology have impacted innumerable literary works, from Shakespeare to J.K. Rowling. Many terms and phrases we use today have their origins in mythology. Greek mythology has influenced the arts for centuries, from ancient Greek sculpture to Renaissance paintings to contemporary movies and television series.

In conclusion, myths were a crucial component of ancient cultures since they served as a tool for moral teaching, cultural transmission, and explanation of the world around them. Greek mythology continues to be popular and has had a significant influence on contemporary society, which is evidence of the strength and importance of these old tales.

- The sources of Greek mythology and their reliability

Greek mythology draws on a wide range of sources, including literature, visual arts, and oral tradition. The works of Homer and Hesiod, who lived in the eighth century BCE, are the earliest extant written sources of Greek mythology. Hesiod's Theogony explains the beginnings of the gods and the world, while Homer's epic poems, the Iliad and the Odyssey, chronicle the tale of the Trojan War and the exploits of the hero Odysseus.

The plays created by the Greek mythology-inspired playwrights Aeschylus, Sophocles, and Euripides are some other significant literary sources of Greek mythology. Ancient Greece had theaters where these plays were presented, and they played a significant role in Greek culture.

Greek mythology was transmitted orally in addition to through written texts. Storytellers, poets, and bards would perform the myths in front of an audience while telling and retelling them. Over time, as different storytellers contributed their own twists and interpretations, these tales were frequently modified and altered.

Greek mythology has a wide range of sources, although academics disagree on whether or not these sources are trustworthy. Greek mythology's oldest recorded sources were frequently created decades after the events they recount, making it difficult to determine how much of the tales are truly legendary and how much is based on historical fact. Additionally, when various storytellers contributed their own twists and interpretations over time, the Greek mythology tales were frequently modified and altered. This implies that the myths that have persisted to the present day may not be the same as those that were first told.

Nevertheless, despite these difficulties, many academics think that the tales of Greek mythology are trustworthy in the sense that they shed light on the attitudes, ideals, and cultural customs of ancient Greece. The tales offer a glimpse into the worldview of the ancient Greeks and were used to impart moral lessons, explain natural phenomena, and influence religious rituals.

Greek mythology's stories have endured for thousands of years, which is evidence of their lasting value and cultural impact. The tales have been told and modified countless times in literature, the arts, and popular culture, and they still enthrall and inspire people today.

In conclusion, Greek mythology draws from a variety of sources, including literature, art, and oral tradition. The stories of Greek mythology offer insight into the beliefs, morals, and cultural practices of ancient Greece, while researchers disagree on the veracity of these sources. Despite the difficulties in interpreting these sources, Greek mythology continues to be significant and influential in culture, which is a monument to its ongoing strength and allure.

Chapter 2: The Creation Myth - The creation of the universe according to Greek mythology

Greek mythology holds that Chaos, a nothingness of gloom and emptiness, existed at the start of the universe's creation. Two primordial gods, Gaia (the Earth) and Uranus (the Sky), who later became the first gods, emerged from Chaos. The Titans, a race of strong, immortal creatures that governed the universe, were then born of Gaia and Uranus.

Cronus, a Titan, deposed his father Uranus and took control of the universe. However, Cronus began to devour his offspring as soon as they were born because of his concern that his own children would one day overthrow him. Zeus was their youngest child, whom his wife Rhea managed to save by hiding him from Cronus and giving him to a foster mother to raise.

Zeus fought the Titans and his father Cronus for supremacy over the universe when he was an adult. Zeus and the other

Olympian gods prevailed in the ensuing struggle, known as the Titanomachy, which lasted ten years. The vanquished Titans were sent to Tartarus, a gloomy realm located under the earth.

Zeus and the other gods took control of the universe when the Titans were vanquished. While his brothers Poseidon and Hades took on the roles of the gods of the sea and the underworld, respectively, Zeus became the ruler of the gods and the deity of the sky. The goddesses also had significant roles in Greek mythology, with Athena standing for knowledge and combat, Aphrodite for beauty and love, and Demeter for fertility and agriculture.

Greek mythology's creation tale reflects how the culture saw the universe and their place in it. The gods and goddesses were viewed as strong, immortal creatures in charge of nature's energies and the destiny of mortals. The beginnings of the world and the natural phenomena that the ancient Greeks saw, such as the cyclical nature of the seasons and the motions of the stars and planets, were also explained by the mythology.

In conclusion, Greek mythology's creation story is a complicated and interesting account of the universe's beginnings and the ascent of the gods and goddesses. The ancient Greeks' conception of the world and their position within it, as well as their ideas regarding the nature of power and the forces of nature, are all reflected in this work. Numerous pieces of literature, artwork, and popular culture have been inspired by the tale of Zeus and the Olympian gods, which is an eternal and enduring component of Western culture.

- The roles of Chaos, Gaia, Uranus, and Cronus

Chaos, Gaia, Uranus, and Cronus are four of the most essential figures in Greek mythology's creation myth. Each of these figures was important in the creation of the universe and the advent of the gods and goddesses.

At the beginning of time, Chaos was the first being to arise from the abyss. Chaos was a shapeless, formless entity that symbolized the universe's primordial state prior to the emergence of order. Chaos was the origin of all creation, as well as the gods and goddesses.

The second creature to emerge from Chaos was Gaia, often known as Mother Earth. Gaia was the earth's personification and the mother of all life. She created mountains, rivers, and oceans, as well as the first generation of gods and goddesses. Uranus, the third entity to arise from Chaos, represented the sky. Uranus was Gaia's husband and the Titans' father. He was an oppressive and ruthless king, and his treatment of his children contributed to their rebellion against him.

Cronus was the Titans' youngest son, the son of Uranus and Gaia. Cronus deposed his father and ascended to the throne of the cosmos. He was a powerful and crafty god, but he was also notorious for his cruelty for devouring his own children. Cronus swallows his children whole in an attempt to keep them from overthrowing him in one well-known tale, but his wife Rhea fools him into eating a stone instead of their youngest kid, Zeus. Zeus eventually defeats Cronus and ascends to the throne of the gods and the cosmos.

In Greek mythology, each of these people played an important role in the creation and structuring of the universe. Chaos symbolized the universe's primordial state before to the formation of order, whereas Gaia was the mother of all life and the source of all creation. Cronus was the powerful and repressive monarch who was eventually ousted by his own children, while Uranus represented the sky and the heavens. These people are significant not only for their roles in the creation story, but also for their influence on Greek mythology in general. The gods and goddesses who arose from these beings went on to become some of Greek mythology's most famous figures, and their stories continue to captivate and inspire people today.

- The birth of the Olympian gods and goddesses

The Olympian gods and goddesses were the most powerful and adored deities in Greek mythology, and their creation is an enthralling story that embodies ancient Greece's culture and beliefs. The Olympian gods and goddesses, according to Greek mythology, were the offspring of Cronus and Rhea, two Titans who governed the universe before the Olympians. Cronus began devouring his progeny as soon as they were born, fearing that they would one day topple him. Rhea, on the other hand, saved their youngest child Zeus by hiding him from Cronus and placing him with a foster mother to nurture. Zeus grew up to become the gods' monarch and the most powerful Olympian.

However, Zeus was not Cronus and Rhea's sole child. They also had five other offspring, Hestia, Demeter, Hera, Poseidon, and Hades, who would become Olympian gods and goddesses. Demeter was the goddess of agriculture and fertility, whereas Hestia was the goddess of the hearth and home. Poseidon was the deity of the sea, whereas Hera was the queen of the gods and the goddess of marriage and childbirth. Hades was the underworld god and ruler of the dead.

However, the emergence of the Olympian gods and goddesses was not without difficulties. Cronus had devoured all of his previous children, and Rhea was determined not to let him do the same to their youngest child. Rhea tricked Cronus by wrapping a stone in swaddling blankets and presenting it to him as their child. Cronus ingested the stone, mistaking it for Zeus, and Rhea was able to conceal her true son from him.

Zeus evolved into a powerful and cunning god, challenging his father Cronus for control of the universe. The ensuing fight, known as the Titanomachy, lasted ten years and was won by Zeus and the other Olympian gods. The Titans were exiled to Tartarus, a dark and foreboding realm beneath the earth. The narrative of the Olympian gods and goddesses' origin reflects the ancient Greeks' view of the world and their place in it. The gods and goddesses were viewed as powerful and immortal creatures who commanded natural forces and decided the fates of mankind. The myths also explained the beginnings of the world and natural phenomena witnessed by the ancient Greeks, such as changing seasons and the movements of the stars and planets.

Finally, the origin of the Olympian gods and goddesses is a fascinating story that depicts ancient Greece's culture and morals. The tale of Zeus and the other Olympian gods has inspired innumerable works of literature, art, and popular culture throughout the centuries. The Olympian gods and goddesses continue to enchant and inspire people today, acting as timeless icons of power, wisdom, and strength.

Chapter 3: The Olympian Gods and Goddesses

- An overview of the Olympian gods and goddesses

The Olympian gods and goddesses are some of Greek mythology's most well-known figures. The Olympian gods and goddesses were thought to reside on Mount Olympus, Greece's highest peak.

Zeus, Hera, Poseidon, Demeter, Athena, Apollo, Artemis, Ares, Aphrodite, Hephaestus, Hermes, and Dionysus were the twelve Olympians. Each of these gods and goddesses had an own realm of influence and were associated with different aspects of life and the natural world.

Zeus was the deity of the sky and thunder, as well as the monarch of the gods. He was the most powerful god, and he was frequently shown wielding a thunderbolt. His wife and sister, Hera, was the goddess of marriage and childbirth, as well as the goddess of jealousy and vengeance.

Poseidon, the god of the sea and earthquakes, was frequently represented with a trident. Demeter was the goddess of agriculture and fertility, and she was in charge of agricultural growth and harvesting.

Athena was the goddess of wisdom, war, and crafts, and she was frequently shown wearing a helmet and wielding a spear. Apollo was associated with the sun and was the god of music, poetry, and prophecy. His twin sister, Artemis, was the goddess of the hunt, the moon, and childbirth.

Ares was the god of war and bloodshed, and he was frequently represented with a spear and shield in his hands. Aphrodite was the goddess of love and beauty who was thought to have been created from sea foam. Hephaestus was the god of fire and metalworking, and he was well-known for his skill.

Hermes was the god of trade and thieves, as well as the messenger of the gods. His sandals and helmet were frequently represented with wings. Dionysus was the deity of wine, festivals, and ecstasy, and was frequently represented holding a drinking cup and surrounded by vine leaves.

The tales of the Olympian gods and goddesses are among the most well-known in Greek mythology. These stories have enthralled people for millennia, from the epic conflicts between Zeus and his siblings to the tales of love and jealousy among the gods and goddesses.

The Olympian gods and goddesses had an essential role in ancient Greek religious activities, in addition to their positions in myth and legend. Throughout the Greek world, temples and shrines were built in their honor, and tributes and sacrifices were given to them in the hope of obtaining their favor.

Finally, the Olympian gods and goddesses are among the most well-known and lasting figures in Greek mythology. Each of these twelve gods and goddesses had their own unique area of influence and played an important role in Greek mythology and legend. Their stories continue to enthrall and inspire people today, and their impact can be seen in art, literature, and popular culture all around the world.

- Their roles and domains of influence

Greek mythology's gods and goddesses were each connected with unique functions and spheres of influence, reflecting the ancient Greeks' understanding of the universe and their place in it. Comprehending these roles and domains is essential for understanding ancient Greek myths and stories.

Zeus was the deity of the sky and thunder, as well as the monarch of the gods. He was commonly shown carrying a thunderbolt and was linked with power, strength, and authority. His wife and sister, Hera, was the queen of the gods as well as the goddess of marriage and childbirth. She was frequently represented as a lovely and royal lady, with a peacock as her symbol.

Poseidon was the sea god, as well as the god of earthquakes and horses. He was frequently portrayed with a trident and was associated with power, unpredictability, and danger. Demeter was the goddess of agriculture and fertility, and she was associated with the harvest and the seasons changing.

She was frequently represented with a sheaf of wheat or a cornucopia.

Hades was the underworld god and ruler of the dead. He was frequently represented as a stern and scary figure, and he was linked to death, darkness, and the hereafter. Athena was the goddess of wisdom and combat, as well as strategy, bravery, and insight. She was frequently shown with a helmet and a spear.

Apollo was associated with music, poetry, prophecy, and healing. He was linked to the arts and was frequently shown with a lyre or a bow and arrow. Artemis was the goddess of the hunt and the moon, and she was connected with nature and the wilderness. Her symbol was a bow and arrow, and she was generally represented as a tough and independent lady.

Aphrodite was the goddess of beauty, love, and sexuality. She was generally shown as a lovely and enticing woman, and was connected with desire, pleasure, and attraction. Hephaestus was the deity of fire and forge, as well as craftsmanship and technology. He was frequently represented as a talented blacksmith at his forge.

Hermes was the gods' messenger, and he was associated with communication, travel, and commerce. He was frequently represented with winged sandals, a winged helmet, and a caduceus. Dionysus was a Greek god who was associated with wine, fertility, and ecstasy. He was connected with inebriation, festivity, and excess, and was frequently shown holding a vine or a wine cup.

The functions and spheres of influence of Greek mythology's gods and goddesses reflect the ancient Greeks' perception of the universe and their place in it. The gods and goddesses were viewed as powerful and immortal creatures who commanded natural forces and decided the fates of mankind. The myths also explained the beginnings of the world and natural phenomena witnessed by the ancient Greeks, such as changing seasons and the movements of the stars and planets.

Finally, the gods and goddesses of Greek mythology each had their own distinct duties and spheres of influence, reflecting the ancient Greeks' understanding of the world and their place within it. Ancient Greek myths and stories continue to captivate and inspire people today, acting as timeless representations of power, wisdom, and strength.

- Famous myths featuring the Olympians, such as the abduction of Persephone

Some of the most well-known and enduring narratives of Greek mythology feature the Olympian gods and goddesses. These stories frequently explore themes of love, jealousy, power, and the human-divine relationship. Here are some instances of well-known mythology involving the Olympians: This tale describes how Hades, the underworld's god, abducted Persephone, daughter of Demeter, and brought her to the underworld to be his bride. Demeter, heartbroken by the death of her daughter, forbade the growth of crops on the earth, resulting in starvation and suffering. Eventually, Zeus intervened and negotiated a bargain whereby Persephone would spend half the year in the underworld with Hades and half the year on earth with her mother, resulting in the seasonal cycle.

Heracles, son of Zeus, was renowned for his extraordinary strength and heroic acts. The accomplishment of twelve labors entrusted to him by King Eurystheus as penance for murdering his own family in a fit of lunacy was one of his most renowned achievements. This entailed killing the Nemean Lion, capturing the Erymanthian Boar, and cleansing the Augean Stables.

Aphrodite, the goddess of love and beauty, fell in love with Adonis, a mortal man renowned for his beauty. The two became lovers, but Adonis was later slain when hunting by a wild boar. Aphrodite, filled with sorrow, transformed Adonis into an anemone flower, which became a symbol of his beauty and tragic end.

The Trojan War: The Trojan War, fought between the Greeks and Trojans over Helen of Troy, is one of the most well-known stories in Greek mythology. The activities of the gods and goddesses, who took sides and engaged in the affairs of mankind, triggered the conflict. The ten-year conflict was marked by epic battles, heroic achievements, and heartbreaking losses.

People have been intrigued by these mythology and numerous more involving the Olympian gods and goddesses for generations. Their themes and motifs continue to resonate with people today, as they continue to be repeated and altered in literature, art, and popular culture. Whether examining the nature of love and jealousy, the relationship between humanity and the divine, or the fight for power and supremacy, the myths involving the Olympians remain among the most enduring and potent tales in human history.

Chapter 4: Heroes and Mortals

- The role of heroes and mortals in Greek mythology

In Greek mythology, heroes and mortals played significant roles as protagonists and symbols of the human predicament. Hercules, Perseus, and Theseus were celebrated for their strength, bravery, and cunning, and were the focus of numerous myths and stories. Mortals, on the other hand, were frequently the victims of the capriciousness of the gods and served as examples of the repercussions of hubris and disobedience.

In Greek mythology, heroes were frequently the offspring of a god or goddess and a human. They possessed exceptional strength, wisdom, or beauty, and were frequently required to complete impossible undertakings or missions. As punishment for murdering his wife and children in a fit of rage, Hercules, who was renowned for his extraordinary strength, was required to complete twelve labors. Perseus was renowned for his intelligence and courage, and was credited with killing the terrifying Gorgon Medusa and saving the princess Andromeda from a sea monster. Theseus, renowned for his wisdom and bravery, was credited with slaying the terrifying Minotaur and liberating Athens from tyranny.

On the other hand, mortals were frequently the victims of the caprice of the gods. They were vulnerable to the whims of fate and fortune and were frequently used to highlight the repercussions of arrogance and disobedience. The story of Icarus, for instance, serves as a cautionary tale against the perils of ambition and recklessness. Icarus and his father Daedalus attempted to escape their enslavement on the island of Crete by fashioning wings out of feathers and wax. Icarus, however, soared too close to the sun, and the heat destroyed his wings, leading him to plummet into the sea and drown.

The tale of Prometheus is another illustration of the perils of disobedience. Prometheus was a Titan who rebelled against the gods' power by stealing fire from them and giving it to humanity. As a punishment, Zeus tied him to a rock and had an eagle peck out his liver each day, only for it to regrow each night. Hercules eventually liberated Prometheus, but the narrative serves as a cautionary tale against defying the gods' authority.

In Greek mythology, the roles of heroes and mortals reflect the ancient Greeks' perception of the human condition. Heroes were viewed as special persons with remarkable talents, and they were frequently required to complete impossible feats or missions. Mortals, on the other hand, were susceptible to the whims of fate and fortune and served as examples of arrogance and disobedience.

In conclusion, heroes and mortals served as both protagonists and emblems of the human predicament in Greek mythology. The myths and legends of ancient Greece continue to fascinate and inspire people, acting as enduring symbols of power, wisdom, and strength, as well as warning tales about the perils of ambition and disobedience.

- Famous heroes such as Hercules, Achilles, and Theseus

Greek mythology is replete with tales of heroes who performed extraordinary deeds and accomplished extraordinary achievements. Numerous of these heroes have achieved literary fame and continue to inspire people today. Here are a few instances of well-known Greek mythology heroes:

Hercules was the son of Zeus and a mortal woman. He is arguably the most well-known of all the Greek heroes. As punishment for murdering his own family in a fit of madness, he was renowned for his tremendous strength and the twelve labors he performed. This entailed killing the Nemean Lion, capturing the Erymanthian Boar, and cleansing the Augean Stables.

Achilles was the greatest Trojan War warrior and the principal character in Homer's epic poem the Iliad. His main weakness was his heel, which rendered him invulnerable. The narrative of Achilles is one of valor and honor, but also of pride and the perils of unbridled ambition.

Theseus was the son of the king of Athens, Aegeus, and is arguably most known for slaying the Minotaur, a monster with the body of a man and the head of a bull. Theseus explored the labyrinth in which the Minotaur resided and slew the beast, therefore liberating Athens from its shackles.

Perseus was the son of the god Zeus and a mortal woman. He is renowned for defeating the Gorgon Medusa, whose glance had the power to turn humans to stone. Perseus was able to chop off Medusa's head with the aid of Athena and Hermes and use it to defeat his adversaries.

Jason was the leader of the Argonauts, who embarked on the ship Argo in pursuit of the Golden Fleece. Jason and his comrades overcame numerous obstacles and fought monsters en route to getting the Golden Fleece and bringing it to Greece, but they were ultimately unsuccessful.

Their bravery, fortitude, and tenacity continue to inspire people to this day, as do those of many others. They reflect the noblest aspects of humanity, such as bravery, honor, and selflessness. Their influence is seen in everything from superhero films to video games.

In addition to their own achievements, these heroes played significant roles in ancient Greek mythology. They communicated with the gods and goddesses, braved the perils of Hades, and helped mold the fate of the Greek world.

The heroes of Greek mythology are, in conclusion, some of the most lasting and inspiring individuals in world literature. From Hercules' amazing strength to Achilles' valor, their tales continue to captivate and inspire people today. These heroes exemplify the finest of humanity and remind us of the strength of courage, honor, and selflessness.

- The concept of the hero's journey and its significance in Greek mythology

The concept of the hero's journey has been employed in narrative for millennia, and it is especially prevalent in Greek mythology. The hero's journey is a narrative structure that describes the hero's route as he or she undertakes a quest or confronts a problem. Joseph Campbell first proposed the concept in his book "The Hero with a Thousand Faces." Since then, it has been a common framework for understanding myths and stories.

The hero's journey is a recurring motif in many of the myths and stories of Greek mythology. Frequently, the hero must undertake an apparently difficult adventure or accomplish a seemingly impossible feat. This quest could involve fighting a monster, rescuing a princess, or acquiring a magical item. Along the route, the hero must conquer barriers and overcome difficulties, with the assistance of allies or magical aid.

In Greek mythology, the hero's journey is crucial because it reflects the ancient Greeks' conception of the universe and their place in it. The Greeks viewed themselves as a part of a broader story, with their lives and experiences comprising a greater cosmic narrative. This notion is reflected in the hero's journey, as the hero's quest is frequently intertwined with wider themes of fate, destiny, and the conflict between good and evil.

Odysseus's journey is one of the most famous examples of the hero's journey in Greek mythology. Odysseus fought in the Trojan War and was renowned for his brilliance and cunning. After the war, he was tasked with returning to Ithaca to reunite with his wife and children. However, he encountered monsters, storms, and treacherous pals on his trek home. Odysseus had numerous obstacles and failures throughout his journey, but he was finally able to overcome them via his intelligence and cunning. He was supported by allies such as the goddess Athena and was intelligent enough to outwit his adversaries. His voyage home involved not just physical travel, but also self-discovery and development.

In Greek mythology, the hero's journey illustrates the significance of tenacity, courage, and resolve in the face of hardship. The hero is frequently viewed as a figure of hope and inspiration, symbolizing the ancient Greeks' most cherished traits and principles. The journey of the hero also represents the major ideas of fate and destiny in the ancient Greek worldview.

The significance of the hero's journey in Greek mythology reflects the ancient Greeks' conception of the universe and their place within it. The hero's journey is a recurring motif in many myths and legends, and it helps to emphasize the significance of perseverance, courage, and resolve in the face of hardship. The hero is a symbol of hope and inspiration, reflecting the ancient Greek worldview's primary virtues and values.

Chapter 5: Monsters and Creatures

- The role of monsters and creatures in Greek mythology

Greek mythology places a lot of emphasis on monsters and animals, which frequently represent chaos, peril, and the unknowable. From the multiheaded Hydra to the half-human, half-animal centaurs, they appear in all sizes and shapes. Here are a few renowned monsters and creatures from Greek mythology, to name just a few:

The Minotaur was a mythical beast with a bull's head and a man's body. It supposedly originated from the coupling of the queen of Crete and a bull and resided in the labyrinth on the island of Crete. The task was given to the hero Theseus, who slew the Minotaur by making it out of the labyrinth.

The Hydra was a creature with many heads that resembled a serpent; anytime one head was removed, two more would grow in its place. It was ultimately vanquished by the hero Heracles, who was able to cauterize the head stumps to stop them from sprouting new heads.

The Chimera was a beast with a lion-like head, a goat-like body, and a serpent-like tail. The hero Bellerophon, who rode the winged horse Pegasus and used his spear to fight the beast, eventually killed it. It breathed fire.

The Cyclops: These enormous, one-eyed animals were thought to be the offspring of the Poseidon-like god. They were renowned for their physical prowess and capacity to craft potent weapons. One well-known myth of the Cyclops is that of Odysseus, who, when stranded on its island, managed to blind the monster Polyphemus in order to flee.

The Sphinx: The Sphinx was a beast with a lion's body and a human head. It presented passengers with puzzles to complete, and if they failed, it would kill them. In one well-known tale, the hero Oedipus managed to crack the Sphinx's code and vanquish the beast.

In Greek mythology, these monsters and creatures represented the unknowable, the perilous, and the chaotic. They served as a metaphor for the elements of nature that were beyond human control and put the courage and cunning of the heroes who battled them to the test. As was the case with the Hydra and the Minotaur, some of the monsters were vanquished by sheer force. In other instances, like with the Sphinx and the Chimera, the heroes had to utilize their wits and ingenuity to vanquish the adversaries.

The monsters and beasts of Greek mythology served a practical function in the stories in addition to their symbolic meaning. They offered the heroes a source of conflict and difficulty, and their defeat frequently signaled a turning point in the hero's path.

In conclusion, Greek mythological monsters and creatures are among the most enduring and iconic characters in all of literature. They serve as metaphors for the uncharted and the perilous, and they put the courage and cunning of the heroes up against them to the test. These creatures, from the many-headed Hydra to the one-eyed Cyclops, still captivate and inspire people today.

- Famous examples such as the Minotaur, Medusa, and the Hydra

Many of the interesting and horrifying animals seen in Greek mythology have become well-known figures in modern culture. These include the Minotaur, Medusa, and the Hydra, each of which has a special tale to tell and qualities that are all their own.

The Minotaur was a beast with a bull's head and a man's body. It kept a regular diet of human sacrifices and dwelt in a labyrinth on the island of Crete. Theseus eventually defeated the Minotaur by navigating the labyrinth and killing the beast with strength and cunning.

A Gorgon with snakes for hair and the ability to transform targets into stone, Medusa was a Gorgon. She was once a stunning woman, but Athena cursed her for defiling her shrine. Perseus, a hero, eventually killed Medusa by cutting off her head after dodging her stare with a mirror.

The Lerna wetlands were home to the multiheaded serpent known as the Hydra. It was claimed to have nine heads, and for every head removed, it could develop two more. Hercules eventually defeated the Hydra, and by cauterizing the wounds with fire, he was able to stop the heads from regrowing.

These well-known figures from Greek mythology provide as potent metaphors for the might and peril of nature. Additionally, they depict the worries and aspirations of the ancient Greeks as well as their perspective of the world and their position within it.

For instance, the Minotaur stands for the perils of unbridled power as well as the value of bravery and fortitude in the face of difficulty. The labyrinth itself is a metaphor for life's complexity and unpredictability, and it highlights the necessity for heroes who can successfully negotiate life's unexpected turns.

Medusa, on the other hand, stands in for the perils of beauty as well as the results of conceit and hubris. Her power to turn humans into stone is a reflection of the ancient Greeks' faith in fate and their understanding of the perils of disobedience.

The Hydra stands for the perils of chaos as well as the value of tenacity and resolve in the face of insurmountable challenges. Ancient Greeks believed in the strength of the will, the value of courage, and the importance of determination. Hercules' ability to defeat the Hydra and stop its heads from coming back is a reflection of this belief.

As a conclusion, the Minotaur, Medusa, and Hydra are only a handful of the numerous amazing and frightful creatures that appear in Greek mythology. The might and danger of the natural world, as well as the ancient Greeks' perception of the world and their place in it, are all powerfully represented by them. Even now, people are still enthralled and moved by these creatures, which are enduring representations of tenacity, bravery, and fortitude.

- The symbolism and significance of these creatures in Greek mythology

Creatures and monsters are interesting beings in Greek mythology, but they also have tremendous symbolism and meaning. The worries and uncertainties of the human experience are embodied in these creatures, which stand in for nature's basic powers. They are frequently portrayed as being erratic and dangerous, testing the strength of the Olympian gods and the courage of the heroes who must confront them. The symbolism and significance of these creatures in Greek mythology are illustrated by the following instances:

The Hydra is a representation of renewal and rebirth. Its capacity to regrow two heads for each head that is amputated symbolizes the never-ending cycle of life and death. The destruction of the Hydra by Heracles, who was able to cauterize the head stumps to stop them from regrow, represents the hero's victory over the forces of chaos.

The Minotaur: The Minotaur is a representation of humanity's animalistic and brutish nature. The dangers of unbridled passions and wants are symbolized by its hideous shape. The victory of reason and civilization over the wild and untamed is symbolized by the hero Theseus' destruction of the Minotaur in the labyrinth.

The Chimera: The Chimera is a representation of the perils of conceit and haughtiness. It violates the natural order and challenges the gods with its bizarre amalgamation of animal components. Bellerophon's victory over the Chimera with the aid of Pegasus is a metaphor for how bravery, creativity, and divine intervention triumph over insurmountable challenges. The Cyclops is a representation of power and savagery. Their one-eyed appearance symbolizes a narrow concentration and a limitation to seeing the big picture. The victory of the hero Odysseus over the Cyclops Polyphemus through guile and strategy represents the superiority of intellect and wit over brute force.

The Sphinx: The Sphinx is a representation of mysticism and wisdom. Its puzzles stand in for life's secrets and the difficulty of comprehending the outside world. By deciphering the Sphinx's riddle, the hero Oedipus defeated it, symbolizing the victory of knowledge and reason over folly and confusion. Greek mythology uses these beings and monsters as powerful metaphors for the forces of nature's origin and the difficulties faced by humans. They oppose the authority of the gods and the valor of the heroes while embodying the anxieties and fears of the human psyche. Their loss frequently serves as a metaphor for how human virtues and ideals prevail against disorder and uncertainty.

In addition, these monsters and beasts also have a practical function in the Greek myths. They serve as a source of tension and challenge for the heroes, motivating them to face their anxieties and constraints and grow into their best selves. They also encourage the heroes and the audience to live with wisdom and restraint by serving as a reminder of the perils of arrogance and unbridled desires.

In conclusion, Greek mythology's monsters and animals are not only interesting creatures but also significant representations of the human experience. The heroes are motivated by them to face their fears and limits and develop into their best selves since they represent the fundamental forces of nature and the difficulties of the human psyche. Their loss serves as a reminder of the value of wisdom and moderation in the face of uncertainty by symbolizing the victory of human values and virtues over chaos and ambiguity.

Chapter 6: The Trojan War

- The story of the Trojan War and its importance in Greek mythology

One of Greek mythology's most well-known and lasting legends is that of the Trojan War. The Greeks and the Trojans engaged in a war that is claimed to have lasted ten years. Numerous retellings and adaptations of the tale have been produced, and it continues to be a potent representation of tragedy and heroism.

Helen, the wife of the Greek king Menelaus, was kidnapped by the Trojan prince Paris, sparking the start of the Trojan War. This was viewed by the Greeks as a serious affront, and they collected their troops to invade Troy. The Greeks besieged the Trojans for ten long years as they battled them on the fields outside of the city.

There were many brave acts and heartbreaking deaths during the war. Along with Achilles, Hector, and Odysseus, many other well-known heroes fought on both sides. The Trojans were eventually routed by the Greeks, who entered the city on a wooden horse.

Greek mythology places a lot of importance on the Trojan War account. It is a potent representation of the influence of fate as well as the results of pride and ambition. The war, which was waged over a woman's love, serves as a warning about the perils of desire and the results of selfishness.

The ancient Greeks' perception of the world and their place in it is also reflected in the war. The Greeks believed that their lives and experiences formed a broader story that included the cosmos as a whole. This perspective is reflected in the Trojan War, which is seen as a component of a wider series of occurrences that mold the world and the lives of those who dwell in it.

Due to the numerous well-known heroes that participated in the Trojan War, the conflict has significance in Greek mythology as well. These heroes represent the qualities and ideals that the Greeks of antiquity cherished, such as bravery, valour, and intelligence. These heroes' tales still enthrall and inspire people today, acting as timeless representations of the human spirit and its capacity to triumph over hardship.

In conclusion, one of Greek mythology's most well-known and enduring narratives is that of the Trojan War. The Greeks' perception of the universe and their place in it are reflected in the war, which stands as a potent emblem of fate's influence and the results of pride and ambition. As representations of the human spirit and its capacity to triumph over adversity, the many well-known heroes who participated in the conflict continue to enthrall and inspire people to this day. The Trojan War tale continues to enthrall and inspire people all around the world, serving as a monument to the enduring power of myth and storytelling.

- The key players, such as Achilles, Agamemnon, and Hector

The Trojan War was fought between the Greeks and the Trojans over the kidnapping of Helen, the wife of Greek King Menelaus. The conflict lasted ten years and was fought by numerous heroes and major actors on both sides. Here are some of the Trojan War's main players:

Achilles: The Iliad's principal figure is Achilles, the greatest warrior of the Greek army. Except for his heel, he was famed for his tremendous strength and invulnerability. Achilles enlisted in the war despite his mother's warnings that he would perish in battle. His devastating defects were his rage and pride, which finally led to his downfall.

Agamemnon was the king of Mycenae and the supreme leader of the Greek army. He was a formidable commander who brought the Greeks together against the Trojans. His arrogance and greed, however, drove him to clash with his fellow Greeks, particularly with Achilles. He stole Achilles' battle prize, the Trojan princess Briseis, forcing Achilles to abandon the war.

Hector: Hector was the Trojan army's best warrior and the protector of Troy. He was well-known for his bravery and devotion to his family and city. Hector was a pivotal figure in the Trojan War, and his death at the hands of Achilles was a watershed moment in the conflict and a tragedy for the Trojans.

Odysseus: Odysseus was a Greek hero noted for his cunning and cleverness. He was a pivotal figure in the Trojan Battle, notably the famous Trojan Horse ploy that allowed the Greeks to enter Troy and win the war. Odysseus was also recognized for his bravery and fighting ability, and he was one of the few Greek heroes to survive and return home after the battle.

Paris: Paris was the Trojan prince who kidnapped Helen and set the Trojan War in motion. He was recognized for his beauty and love for Helen, but also for his fear and inability to fight. Paris was a divisive figure during the Trojan War since his actions resulted in the deaths of many individuals on both sides.

Helen was Menelaus' wife and the catalyst for the Trojan War. She was famous for her beauty and her position as the world's most attractive lady. Helen was kidnapped by Paris and carried to Troy, prompting the Greeks to attack the city. Helen was a tragic figure, despite her role in the war, because her beauty allowed her to be objectified and used as a pawn by the men around her.

Each of the Trojan War's important characters had their own set of talents, flaws, and motivations. Achilles was the best warrior in the Greek army, but his arrogance proved his undoing. Agamemnon was a strong leader, but his hubris and avarice prompted him to clash with his fellow Greeks. Hector was the Trojan army's strongest warrior, and his love for his family and hometown made him a sympathetic figure. Odysseus was a hero noted for his cunning and intelligence, and his role in the Trojan War was critical to the Greek victory. Paris and Helen were divisive figures since their acts resulted in the deaths of many people and extensive suffering.

Finally, the primary players in the Trojan War were multifaceted individuals with varying talents, flaws, and goals. They represented the war's various viewpoints and perspectives, and their actions influenced the conflict's outcome. Despite their imperfections, these personalities continue to intrigue and inspire people today, and their stories remind us of the human cost of war and the complexities of the human experience.

- The aftermath of the war and its impact on Greek mythology

The Trojan War's aftermath had a tremendous impact on Greek mythology. The war itself was a protracted and cruel fight that claimed the lives of many warriors and civilians. However, the war's consequences did not cease with the end of hostilities.

The emergence of new myths and stories was one of the most significant effects of the battle. The Trojan War and its heroes' legends were passed down through generations, generating innumerable retellings and adaptations. The war became a defining moment in Greek mythology, symbolizing fate's might and the consequences of ambition.

The conflict also had a tremendous impact on Greek mythology's gods and goddesses. The gods were strongly involved in the war, choosing sides and interfering. The actions of the gods throughout the conflict were interpreted as reflections of their personalities and motivations, and they served to reaffirm the ancient Greeks' view of the world and their place in it.

In the aftermath of the conflict, new heroes and legends emerged. The epic poem "The Odyssey" was inspired by the stories of Odysseus and his ten-year journey home. The narrative of Agamemnon and his family inspired several myths and stories, notably the renowned tragedy "The Oresteia."

The war also influenced the ancient Greeks' view of their own history and identity. The conflict was regarded as a watershed point in Greek history, acting as a symbol of the Greeks' tenacity and fortitude in the face of adversity. The Greeks considered themselves as the offspring of the battle heroes, and the conflict became an important element of their cultural identity.

The war's aftermath had a significant impact on the ancient Greeks' perspective of the world around them. The conflict was viewed as a reflection of bigger forces shaping the world, such as fate, destiny, and the struggle between good and evil. The war became a metaphor for the wider obstacles and struggles that the ancient Greeks encountered, and it served as a reminder of the value of perseverance, resolve, and fortitude in the face of adversity.

Finally, the consequences of the Trojan War had a tremendous impact on Greek mythology. The conflict itself became a defining episode in Greek history, symbolizing the Greeks' tenacity and resilience in the face of adversity. The conflict also had a significant impact on Greek mythology's gods and goddesses, as well as the heroes and legends that flourished in its aftermath. The war became a metaphor for the wider obstacles and struggles that the ancient Greeks encountered, and it served as a reminder of the value of perseverance, resolve, and fortitude in the face of adversity.

Chapter 7: Love and Relationships

- The role of love and relationships in Greek mythology

In Greek mythology, love and relationships shape the tales of gods, heroes, and mortals. In Greek mythology, love is frequently portrayed as a potent force capable of inciting intense emotion, loyalty, and tragedy. Here are some instances where love and relationships played a significant role in Greek mythology:

The relationship between Zeus, the king of the gods, and Hera, his queen, was marred by infidelity and jealousy. Despite their disagreements, their partnership represented the significance of marriage and family in Greek culture.

Aphrodite and Adonis: The goddess of love, Aphrodite, fell in love with the mortal hunter, Adonis. As Adonis was murdered by a wild boar, their relationship was passionate but brief. The tragic tale of Aphrodite and Adonis illustrates the impermanence of love and the inevitability of death.

Orpheus, a great musician, fell in love with Eurydice, but she passed very shortly after their wedding. Orpheus journeyed to the underworld to beg Hades to return her to the land of the living, and he was granted permission to do so as long as he did not look back at her. However, he breached his word and Eurydice was lost forever. The tale of Orpheus and Eurydice is a painful reminder of the strength of love and the repercussions of broken promises.

Pyramus and Thisbe: Pyramus and Thisbe were two lovers whose parents prohibited them from marrying. When they decided to elope, tragedy befell them. Pyramus incorrectly assumed Thisbe had been killed by a lion and committed suicide, while Thisbe, upon discovering Pyramus dead, also committed suicide. The tragic tale of Pyramus and Thisbe is a famous depiction of forbidden love.

These tales of love and relationships from Greek mythology demonstrate the strength and complexity of human emotions. However, love can also result in tragedy and heartache. As mortals attempt to navigate the power dynamics and expectations of their supernatural counterparts, relationships between mortals and gods are typically fraught with danger and strife.

In addition, these love and relationship narratives serve as a mirror of Greek culture and its values. Marriage and family were highly regarded in ancient Greek culture, and Zeus and Hera's connection was viewed as a symbol of their significance. The forbidden love stories, such as Pyramus and Thisbe, illustrate the rigid social rules and taboos of ancient Greek culture.

In conclusion, love and relationships have a complicated and multidimensional role in Greek mythology. Love is portrayed as a potent energy that may inspire enormous passion and devotion, but also tragedy and heartache. Relationships between people and gods are frequently laden with peril and strife, reflecting the power structure and expectations of Greek society. These love and relationship narratives continue to intrigue and inspire people, reminding us of the eternal strength and complexity of human emotions.

- Famous examples such as the love story of Orpheus and Eurydice

Orpheus and Eurydice's love story is one of the most renowned examples of love and relationships in Greek mythology. Orpheus was a famous musician and poet, and Eurydice was his adoring wife. Theirs is a moving narrative of love, tragedy, and the power of music.

Orpheus and Eurydice were madly in love, but their joy was fleeting. Eurydice died shortly after their wedding after being bitten by a snake. Orpheus was grieved by her death and determined to journey to the underworld to beg Hades, the god of the dead, to resurrect her.

Orpheus, armed solely with his lyre, performed a melancholy music that stirred the gods and the spirits of the dead. Hades was so captivated by his music that he decided to let Eurydice return to the land of the living on the condition that Orpheus not glance back at her until they were in the world of the living.

Orpheus and Eurydice began their journey back to the world of the living, but Orpheus couldn't stop himself from looking back at his loving bride. Eurydice vanished forever as he turned to look at her, swallowed up by the darkness of the abyss. Orpheus was alone and heartbroken, his music muffled by the death of his love.

The tragic tale of Orpheus and Eurydice is about the power of love and the consequences of breaking promises. It's also a fable about music's ability to move gods and express human feelings.

Orpheus was a mythological musician and poet whose music was thought to have the power to move stones and trees. His music reflected his feelings for Eurydice, and it was his music that convinced the gods to let him try to resurrect her. However, it was his love that drove him to breach his commitment and return to his cherished wife, resulting in her everlasting loss.

Throughout history, the narrative of Orpheus and Eurydice has inspired innumerable artists and writers. From Ovid's Metamorphoses to Cocteau's Orphée, it has been retold in numerous works of literature, music, and art. It has also sparked various adaptations and variants, notably Jean Anouilh's and Sarah Ruhl's plays Eurydice.

Orpheus and Eurydice's narrative is a timeless and universal tale about the power of love and the repercussions of breaking promises. It serves as a reminder that while love can elicit immense passion and dedication, it can also result in tragedy and heartache. It is also a testament to music's ability to articulate human emotions and move the gods themselves. Finally, Orpheus and Eurydice's love story is one of the most famous examples of love and relationships in Greek mythology. It's a tragic story about the power of love and the consequences of broken vows, as well as a testament to music's ability to portray human emotions. Throughout history, the story has inspired innumerable artists and writers, and it remains a timeless and universal tale of the eternal force and complexities of human emotions.

- The symbolism and significance of these stories in Greek mythology

Greek mythology's stories are rich in symbolism and meaning, acting as potent allegories for the human experience. These stories are filled with larger-than-life characters and epic struggles, each of which represents a different aspect of the human condition or the natural world.

The concept of fate and destiny is one of the most important motifs in Greek mythology. The ancient Greeks believed fate was an unavoidable force that regulated the lives of all people, from the most insignificant mortal to the most powerful god. Greek mythology is replete of characters who are subject to the whims of fate and must overcome the barriers that fate sets in their path.

The concept of hubris, or inordinate pride, is another key motif in Greek mythology. The Greeks saw hubris as a deadly and destructive energy that might bring down even the most powerful people. Many Greek mythological myths serve as cautionary tales about the pitfalls of arrogance and the value of humility and respect for the gods.

In Greek mythology, the gods themselves are important symbols. Each god and goddess represents a different facet of the natural world or the human experience, and they all serve as strong metaphors for the forces that form our existence. The gods' stories are full of drama and conflict, reflecting the ancient Greeks' view of the world as one of perpetual battle and change.

Greek mythology's stories also reflect the ancient Greeks' sense of themselves and their place in the universe. These stories are full with heroes and heroines who exemplify the traits and values held important by the ancient Greeks, such as courage, strength, and intelligence. These heroes are compelling representations of the human spirit and its ability to triumph against hardship.

Finally, Greek mythology stories are remarkable because of their continuing power and effect. These stories have been passed down from generation to generation, inspiring numerous works of art, literature, and music. The myths and tales of ancient Greece have become a part of the Western world's cultural history, acting as a compelling reminder of the enduring power of myth and storytelling.

Finally, the stories of Greek mythology are rich in symbolism and significance, and they serve as potent allegories for the human experience. These myths are rich with symbols, such as fate, hubris, and the gods themselves. Greek mythology's stories represent the ancient Greeks' knowledge of themselves and their place in the universe, and they serve as a reminder of myth's enduring power. Ancient Greek myths and stories continue to inspire and captivate people today, demonstrating the eternal power of the human imagination.

Chapter 8: The Underworld

- The Greek concept of the afterlife and the underworld

The ancient Greeks had a fascinating and sophisticated understanding of the afterlife and the underworld. After death, the souls of the deceased would travel to the underworld, a dark and mysterious realm controlled by the god Hades, according to Greek mythology.

The Greek underworld was a mysterious and terrible place full with unusual and terrifying animals. Cerberus, the three-headed hound who guarded the entrance to the Hades, was the most renowned of these. The Furies, vengeful spirits that punished the wicked, and the judges of the dead, who decided the fate of each soul that entered the realm, also lived in the underworld.

The underworld was divided into regions, each of which was destined for souls with varied fates. The Asphodel Fields were destined for the souls of the common dead, while the Elysian

Fields were reserved for the heroic and righteous. Tartarus was the underworld's deepest and darkest region, reserved for the most wicked and malevolent souls.

For numerous reasons, the concept of the afterlife and the underworld was important in ancient Greek civilization. For starters, it served as a poignant reminder of the fleeting nature of human life and the need of leading a noble and heroic life. Only those who lived a life of courage and decency, the Greeks believed, would be rewarded in the hereafter, while those who were evil or cowardly would be punished.

The underworld notion also reflected the ancient Greeks' knowledge of the natural world. The underworld was seen as a strange and perilous domain teeming with unknown and scary entities. This represented the ancient Greeks' view of the world as one of continual struggle and change, with danger and uncertainty lurking around every corner.

The afterlife and the underworld were also major concepts in Greek mythology and literature. Many of Greek literature's great masterpieces, like the Odyssey, dealt with the themes of death and the afterlife. These stories frequently acted as allegories for the human experience, delving into topics like the nature of heroism, the power of fate, and the conflict between good and evil.

Finally, the Greek concept of the afterlife and the underworld was a complicated and intriguing aspect of Greek society and mythology. The underworld was a mysterious and terrible place full with unusual and terrifying animals. The idea of the afterlife and the underworld acted as a compelling reminder of the fleeting nature of human life and the need of leading a virtuous and heroic life. It was also a significant part of Greek literature and mythology, reflecting the ancient Greeks' perception of the natural world. The concept of the afterlife and the underworld is a profound and persistent aspect of Western cultural tradition.

- The role of Hades, Persephone, and Charon in Greek mythology

Hades, Persephone, and Charon are three Greek mythological beings associated with the underworld and the afterlife. Their responsibilities are linked, and each is crucial in the myths and beliefs about death and the afterlife.

Hades is the underworld god and ruler of the dead. He is frequently represented as a solemn figure, and his name has come to be associated with the hereafter. Hades was one of three brothers who vanquished the Titans and became world rulers. He drew the short straw and became lord of the underworld, a land inhabited by the dead.

Persephone is the goddess of the underworld and the daughter of Demeter, the goddess of the harvest. According to one version of the myth, Hades kidnapped Persephone and carried her to the underworld to become his queen. Demeter was heartbroken by her daughter's death and refused to let anything grow on Earth until Persephone was returned to her. A compromise was eventually found, and Persephone was allowed to spend six months of the year on earth with her mother and six months in the underworld with Hades.

Charon is the ferryman who takes the souls of the deceased across the river Styx, which separates the living and the dead worlds. According to legend, the dead must pay Charon a price to cross the river, and those who cannot pay are sentenced to roam the river's banks for a hundred years. Hades, Persephone, and Charon all play major parts in Greek mythology's myths and beliefs about death and the afterlife. Hades is the underworld's king, and his name has come to represent death and the afterlife. Persephone is associated with the underworld as a queen and a symbol of the life-death cycle. Her story also highlights the significance of harvesting and the shifting of the seasons. Charon is the ferryman who takes the souls of the deceased across the Styx River, and his function highlights the significance of paying respect and honor to the dead.

Many parts of Greek culture and society have been influenced by the beliefs and stories surrounding Hades, Persephone, and Charon. The afterlife, according to the ancient Greeks, was a shadowy region ruled by Hades, and the deceased required the assistance of Charon to cross the river Styx. The narrative of Persephone also highlights the significance of the harvest and the shifting of the seasons, which were critical to Greek society's survival.

Finally, Hades, Persephone, and Charon all play major parts in Greek mythology's myths and beliefs about death and the underworld. Hades is the underworld's king, Persephone is a queen and a symbol of the cycle of life and death, and Charon is the ferryman who takes the souls of the dead across the river Styx. These figures, taken together, represent the significance of death and the afterlife in Greek society, as well as the necessity of paying respect and tribute to the dead. People are still fascinated and inspired by these stories, which serve as a reminder of the continuing strength and complexity of human ideas and myths.

- Famous myths featuring the underworld, such as the story of Orpheus and Eurydice

The underworld was a prominent and persistent aspect of Greek mythology, and it was portrayed in many great myths and legends. The narrative of Orpheus and Eurydice is one of the most well-known stories about the underworld.

Orpheus was a mythological musician and poet known for his seductive melodies and ability to seduce even the gods.

Orpheus fell in love with Eurydice, a lovely nymph, one day. They married soon after, and their love was the envy of everyone who knew them.

Their joy, however, was fleeting. Eurydice perished after being bitten by a deadly snake on their wedding day. Orpheus was heartbroken, and he vowed to travel to the underworld to resurrect her.

Orpheus journeyed to the underworld, accompanied by his lyre and lovely music. He enchanted the Furies and the judges of the dead, and was eventually allowed an audience with Hades and Persephone, the underworld's rulers.

Orpheus implored Hades and Persephone to let him return Eurydice to the living world. They consented to his request, moved by his song and his love for Eurydice, on the condition that he not look back at her until they had departed the underworld.

Orpheus and Eurydice set off on their trip back to the land of the living, but as they neared the surface, Orpheus couldn't resist the urge to look back at his beloved. Eurydice was dragged back into the abyss as he turned, eternally lost to him.

Orpheus and Eurydice's story is a strong allegory for the human experience, examining themes such as the power of love, the inevitability of death, and the frailty of human existence. It also acts as a reminder of the risks of temptation and the value of self-control.

The story of Theseus and the Minotaur is another well-known myth about the underworld. The Athenians were forced to send seven young men and seven young women to Crete every year to be sacrificed to the Minotaur, a frightening creature who resided in a labyrinth beneath the island, according to the story. The son of the Athenian ruler, Theseus, volunteered to be one of the offerings, vowing to fight the Minotaur and put a stop to the sacrifices once and for all. Theseus arrived in Crete, armed with a sword and a ball of thread, and entered the labyrinth. He followed the thread through the labyrinth until he found and killed the Minotaur. He then used the thread to navigate his way out of the labyrinth and returned to Athens, where he was celebrated as a hero. The myth of Theseus and the Minotaur is a potent metaphor of the conflict between good and evil, as well as the importance of perseverance and courage in the face of hardship. It also serves as a warning of the perils of arrogance and the value of humility and reverence for the gods.

Finally, the underworld was a powerful and persistent aspect of Greek mythology, and it was portrayed in many great myths and legends. The legends of Orpheus and Eurydice and Theseus and the Minotaur are only two of numerous myths that deal with death, love, and the conflict between good and evil. These stories continue to inspire and captivate people today as powerful and enduring representations of the human experience.

Chapter 9: The Twelve Labors of Hercules

- The story of Hercules and his twelve labors

Hercules and his twelve labors is one of the most well-known Greek myths. Hercules was the son of Zeus and a mortal woman named Alcmene. He was a powerful warrior and a hero, but he was also notorious for his fury and propensity for violence.

Hercules' woes began when the goddess Hera, who despised him because he was the illegitimate son of her husband Zeus, drove him insane. When Hercules regained his senses and understood what he had done, he was overcome with regret for killing his wife and children.

Hercules was given twelve impossible duties, known as the Labors of Hercules, as penance for his crimes. Hercules was resolved to prove his worthiness for redemption despite the impossibility of completing these challenges.

The first task was to kill the Nemean lion, a formidable creature with impenetrable skin. Hercules was able to strangle the lion with his bare hands and skin it with the animal's own claws.

The second task was to slay the nine-headed Hydra, a monster with the ability to sprout two heads for each one that was severed. Together, Hercules and his nephew, Iolaus, were able to defeat the Hydra by cauterizing its neck stumps with fire to prevent the growth of additional heads.

The third labor consisted of capturing the precious, goddess-protected Golden Hind of Artemis. Hercules was able to capture the deer by tracking it for a year and then luring it into a net.

The fourth labor was to capture the Erymanthian Boar, a monstrous feral pig that terrorized the area. Hercules was able to capture the boar alive after pursuing it into a snowdrift.

The sixth task was to clean the Augean stables, which were filthy and had not been cleaned for years. Hercules rerouted a river so that the filth could be washed away in a single day.

The remaining seven labors consisted of capturing a man-eating horse, defeating a giant bird, stealing the girdle of Hippolyta, queen of the Amazons, capturing the cattle of Geryon, stealing the apples of the Hesperides, capturing Cerberus, the three-headed dog that guarded the entrance to Hades, and cleaning the Stymphalian birds from Lake Stymphaalia.

Hercules accomplished all twelve labors, demonstrating his strength, bravery, and resolve. His tale has inspired numerous works of art and literature, and his name has become synonymous with courage and valor.

In conclusion, the story of Hercules and his twelve labors is a famous Greek mythological tale of courage and salvation. Hercules was driven insane by the goddess Hera and committed heinous atrocities, but he was able to make amends by doing twelve impossible undertakings. His life exemplifies the significance of fortitude, resolve, and bravery in the face of hardship, and his name has become a symbol of valor and perseverance.

- The symbolism and significance of these labors in Greek mythology

The twelve labors of Heracles, often known as Hercules, is one of the most influential and enduring episodes in Greek mythology. Collectively, these labors serve as a potent reminder of the hero's journey and the human experience, with each labor representing a significant symbol or allegory. Heracles's first task was to kill the Nemean Lion, a formidable and deadly beast that could not be killed with mortal weapons. Heracles' victory over the lion symbolizes the significance of strength and perseverance in the face of adversity, as the lion represents the problems and hurdles we face in life.

The second labor was to kill the Hydra, a multi-headed serpent capable of regenerating its severed heads. Heracles' victory against the Hydra symbolizes the value of perseverance and ingenuity in the face of seemingly insurmountable obstacles, while the Hydra represents the insidious nature of evil.

The third task required the capture of the Golden Hind, a sacred animal to the goddess Artemis. The deer symbolizes the chase of elusive ambitions and desires, and Heracles' successful capture of the Golden Hind emphasizes the significance of concentration and perseverance in reaching our objectives.

The fourth labor was to catch the Erymanthian Boar, a ferocious and formidable creature that resided on Mount Erymanthos. Heracles' victory over the boar symbolizes the significance of strength and discipline in the face of disorder and unpredictability, as the boar represents the world's wild and untamed nature.

The fifth work was to clean the manure-filled Augean Stables, which had accumulated over many years. Heracles' accomplishment in cleaning the stables symbolizes the value of hard labor and perseverance, as the stables reflect the need to confront and conquer the filth and difficulties of daily life.

The sixth task was to kill the Stymphalian Birds, a swarm of man-eating birds with metal feathers and vicious beaks. Heracles' victory over the birds symbolizes the significance of self-control and discipline. The birds represent the perils and temptations that we confront in life.

The seventh task was to catch the Cretan Bull, a ferocious and destructive beast that had been tormenting Crete. The bull signifies the necessity to confront and overcome forces of chaos and devastation, and Heracles's ability to capture it symbolizes the significance of courage and resolve in the face of peril.

The seventh labor was to capture Diomedes' man-eating mares, a pack of wild and vicious horses. The horses represent the might and unpredictability of nature, and Heracles' victory over them emphasizes the significance of strength and skill in taming nature.

The eighth task was to acquire the girdle of Hippolyta, the Amazon queen. Heracles' successful acquisition of the girdle illustrates the significance of diplomacy and negotiation in obtaining our objectives, as the girdle signifies the power and authority that accompany leadership.

The eleventh task entailed capturing the livestock of Geryon, a three-headed monster that resided on an island in the Western Ocean. Heracles' victory over Geryon illustrates the significance of resourcefulness and inventiveness in conquering barriers. The cattle represent the wealth and prosperity that may be obtained through hard work and endurance.

The twelfth task was to get the golden apples of the Hesperides, which were protected by a ferocious serpent. The apples signify the benefits and treasures that can be obtained by hard effort and patience, and Heracles' achievement in acquiring them represents the significance of tenacity and dedication in the pursuit of our goals.

The final and twelfth task consisted of capturing Cerberus, the three-headed dog that guarded the gateway to Hades. Heracles' victory over Cerberus depicts the significance of courage and resolve in the face of death and the unknown. Cerberus represents the fear and uncertainty that we experience in life.

In conclusion, the twelve labors of Heracles are rich in symbolism and importance, acting as potent allegories for the journey of the hero and the human experience. Collectively, the labors serve as a reminder of the significance of courage, dedication, endurance, and self-control in conquering life's challenges and hurdles. The labors of Heracles continue to be a potent and enduring element of the Western world's cultural history, inspiring and enthralling people of all ages for generations.

- The impact of Hercules on Greek mythology and culture

Hercules, sometimes known as Heracles, was a pivotal figure in Greek mythology and culture. His story had a great effect on the mythologies and culture of ancient Greece, as well as on succeeding generations.

Hercules represented strength, bravery, and perseverance. He was a warrior and a hero famed for his feats of strength and ability to overcome challenges that seemed insurmountable. His twelve labors have become legendary and continue to inspire others as a testament to the power of perseverance and effort.

In addition to his physical prowess, Hercules represented redemption. His narrative demonstrates the significance of atonement and the potential of salvation, even in the face of heinous acts. This concept is important to numerous Greek stories, and it continues to resonate with modern audiences as a reminder of the power of forgiveness and the potential of second chances.

The influence of Hercules on Greek culture can be observed in numerous parts of society. In many regions of ancient Greece, he was revered as a deity, and his temples and shrines were among the most significant religious places. His image appeared in art, literature, and drama, and he was a favorite topic for poets, playwrights, and visual artists.

The legend of Hercules has also left an indelible mark on Western civilization. His image has appeared in paintings, sculptures, and other artworks, and his name has been exploited to market everything from muscle-building products to amusement parks. His story has been recounted in innumerable literary and cinematic works, and his name has become synonymous with courage and valor.

Hercules has also had a substantial impact on mythology, in addition to his cultural influence. His myth continues to inspire fresh generations of storytellers and mythmakers. His story has also impacted the creation of other myths and legends, and it has helped shape how people view heroes and valor. Hercules was, in conclusion, one of the most important people in Greek mythology and culture. His story had a great effect on the mythologies and culture of ancient Greece, as well as on succeeding generations. His picture and name have become synonymous with courage and valor, and his story continues to inspire people as a monument to the power of perseverance and diligence. His impact on culture and society will continue to be felt by future generations.

Chapter 10: The Legacy of Greek Mythology

- The enduring legacy of Greek mythology in modern culture

Greek mythology has had a significant and persistent influence on contemporary society, affecting everything from music and movies to literature and art. Generations of artists and writers have drawn inspiration and creativity from the tales of the gods and heroes of ancient Greece, which continue to enthrall and inspire people all over the world.

Through literature, Greek mythology has had a tremendous impact on contemporary culture. The themes and motifs of Greek mythology have impacted many of the greatest works of Western literature, from Shakespeare to James Joyce. The Iliad and the Odyssey are just two of Homer's epic writings that have had a particularly significant influence, helping to establish the Western literary canon and inspiring innumerable authors throughout time.

Numerous painters, sculptors, and architects throughout history have drawn inspiration from Greek mythology, which has also had a profound influence on the visual arts. With its emphasis on harmony, symmetry, and proportion, the classical aesthetic of ancient Greece continues to have a significant influence on modern art and design. Ancient Greek monuments and structures like the Parthenon and the Venus de Milo still evoke wonder and adoration in both artists and art enthusiasts.

Greek mythology has had a huge influence on movies and television in popular culture. From Jason and the Argonauts to Clash of the Titans, innumerable films and television programs have based their plots on the exploits of the gods and heroes of ancient Greece. With their tales of bravery, adventure, and romance, these stories continue to enthrall audiences and have influenced how people see what it means to be a hero. Greek mythology has also had an impact on music, with numerous composers finding inspiration in the tales and figures of classical Greece. Greek philosophy, which in turn was influenced by Zarathustra in Nietzsche's book, served as the basis for Richard Strauss' "Also sprach Zarathustra" song. The Roman fable of Lucretia, which has its origins in Greek mythology, served as the inspiration for Benjamin Britten's "The Rape of Lucretia." Greek mythology has impacted even contemporary pop music, with artists like Imagine Dragons and Panic! At The Disco making references to the gods and heroes of classical Greece in their lyrics.

Through its influence on language and literature, Greek mythology has also had a big influence on popular culture. Greek mythology is the source of many English terms and phrases, like "herculean" and "opening Pandora's box." These allusions act as a potent reminder of Greek mythology's continuing influence on our culture and the themes and motifs that continue to resonate in modern life.

In conclusion, Greek mythology's lasting influence on contemporary culture is evidence of the strength and enduring allure of these ageless tales. Greek mythology has shaped our idea of what it is to be human and impacted generations of artists and authors, inspiring everything from literature and art to music and movies. With their stories of bravery, adventure, and romance, the gods and heroes of ancient Greece continue to inspire and enthrall us. They serve as a reminder of the ageless force of myth and the enduring significance of human experience.

- The influence of Greek mythology on literature, art, and popular culture

Greek mythology has had a significant and enduring impact on popular culture, literature, and the arts. Greek myths have been repeated and reinterpreted many times throughout history, and their themes and symbolism are still relevant to people today.

Greek mythology has served as a rich inspiration for writers of many genres and eras in literature. A few instances of how Greek mythology influenced literature are the epic poems of Homer, the tragedies of Sophocles, and the comedies of Aristophanes. Greek mythology is also included into many well-known literary works, such as Shakespeare's "Hamlet" and Milton's "Paradise Lost," in their stories.

Greek mythology has long been a favorite subject for sculptors, painters, and other artists. Greek mythology's gods and goddesses have been portrayed in many works of art, ranging from the Parthenon's ancient sculptures to the Renaissance's paintings. Greek mythology has also served as a source of inspiration for new works of art, including Salvador Dali's surrealist paintings and Jack Kirby's comic book illustrations.

Greek mythology has had a big influence on everything from music to film to fashion in popular culture. Greek mythology has been referred to in many popular songs, including Beyonce's "Halo" and Led Zeppelin's "Achilles Last Stand." Greek mythology has also been a well-liked topic in cinema and television, with works like "Clash of the Titans" and "Xena: Warrior Princess" utilizing its themes and characters. Greek mythology has served as a fashion designer's source of inspiration, with motifs like the Medusa head showing up in everything from apparel to accessories.

Greek mythology's enduring appeal can be linked to its ageless themes and symbolism. Greek mythology's gods and goddesses' tales tackle universal concepts like love, lust, retaliation, and betrayal. The flawed and nuanced characters in these tales are still relatable to people today because of their struggles and victories. The trident of Poseidon and Hermes' winged sandals are two examples of Greek mythology emblems that have evolved into famous designs. Greek mythology has had a profound impact on people's conceptions of the world and their place in it, in addition to literature, art, and popular culture. Greek mythological tales provide an inventive and profound lens through which to view both the natural world and human experience. They offer a foundation for delving into the intricacies of interpersonal relationships, the might of nature, and the unsolved questions of the cosmos.

Greek mythology has, in summary, had a significant and enduring impact on literature, art, and popular culture. Greek myths have been repeated and reinterpreted many times throughout history, and their themes and symbolism are still relevant to people today. Greek mythology's enduring appeal might be traced to its enduring themes and symbols, which present an inventive and profound way of comprehending the universe. Generations to come will continue to be affected by its effects on culture and society.

- Reflections on the importance of Greek mythology in understanding human nature

Greek mythology has long been regarded as a valuable resource for understanding human nature and the inner workings of the human psyche. Ancient Greek myths about the gods and heroes weave a rich tapestry of allegory and symbolism that explores concepts like love, envy, power, and morality. We can learn more about the human condition and the factors that influence us by studying these stories.

The conflict between fate and free will is one of the main themes in Greek mythology. Ancient Greek deities were frequently characterized as arbitrary and unpredictable, treating mortal life as toys at their whim. An essential part of the human experience is this sensation of uncertainty and helplessness in the face of uncontrollable circumstances. The myths of the Greek gods and heroes can aid us in coping with this unpredictability by serving as a reminder that, despite our inability to influence the outside factors that affect our lives, we do have agency and the power to direct our own course of events.

Greek mythology also addresses the nature of power and its corrupting effects. Ancient Greek myths about the gods and heroes frequently discuss the negative effects of uncontrolled power and the perils of hubris. For instance, the tale of Icarus serves as a cautionary tale about the perils of overreaching and the pursuit of power at any costs. The myth of Narcissus, on the other hand, examines the perils of excessive self-absorption and the destructive nature of self-obsession.

Another major topic in Greek mythology is love, and there are many stories of passion, jealousy, and heartbreak to be found in the tales of the gods and heroes of ancient Greece. These tales shed light on the complexities of love relationships and the numerous variables that can affect our choices in partners.

They also serve as a reminder of how love can motivate and encourage us despite severe adversity.

Last but not least, Greek mythology provides us with a rich tapestry of allegory and symbolism that can aid us in comprehending the basic characteristics of the human experience. Ancient Greek myths about the gods and heroes are replete with potent archetypes and symbols, from the sage and strong Athena to the passionate and impulsive Apollo. These archetypes represent facets of our individual personalities and can aid in our quest for a deeper understanding of both.

Finally, Greek mythology is a rich and reliable source of understanding the complexity of human nature and the human experience. We can comprehend the underlying themes and motifs that influence our lives better by studying the tales of the Greek gods and heroes. These themes and motifs range from the conflict between fate and free will to the nature of power and the complexity of love. These tales' ongoing appeal is evidence of both their eternal relevance and the myth's unfailing capacity to uplift and enlighten us.

Printed in Great Britain
by Amazon